FAMILIES of Fame & Fortune

THE JONAS BROTHERS

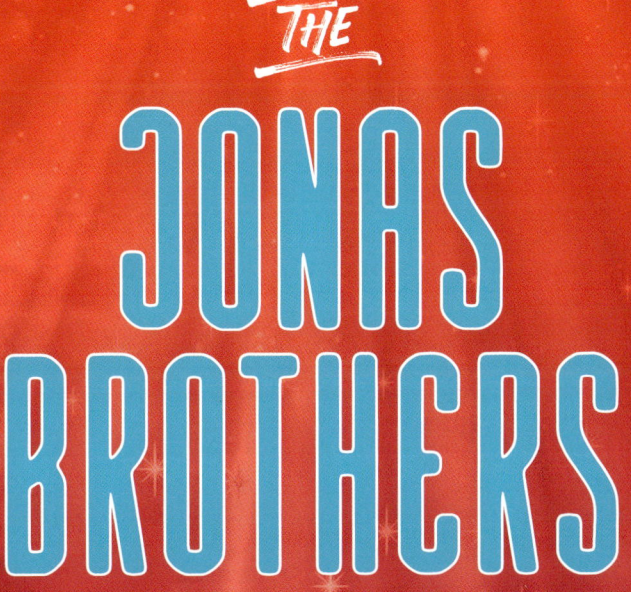

by Kristin J. Russo

For Lauren, who loved people of all walks of life, and relished hearing their stories.

The Jonas Brothers
Families of Fame and Fortune

Copyright © 2021
Published by Full Tilt Press
Written by Kristin J. Russo
All rights reserved.

Printed in the United States of America.
No part of this book may be reproduced in any manner whatsoever without written permission, except in the case of brief quotations embodied in critical articles and reviews.

Full Tilt Press
42964 Osgood Road
Fremont, CA 94539
readfulltilt.com

Full Tilt Press publications may be purchased for educational, business, or sales promotional use.

Editorial Credits
Design and layout by Sara Radka
Edited by Renae Gilles
Copyedited by Nikki Ramsay

Image Credits
Getty Images: Amy Sussman, 25 (top), Brian Babineau, 15, dcp/Kevin Winter, cover, Ethan Miller, 17 (bottom), Frazer Harrison, 3 (bottom), 9, 11, 12 (left), 13 (left), 17 (top), 19, 20 (top), 20 (bottom), 27 (top), 28 (left), Frederick M. Brown, 26 (top), Global Citizen/Noam Galai, 27 (bottom), Imeh Akpanudosen, 26 (bottom), 28 (right), Jamie McCarthy, 16, 24, Kevin Winter, 13 (right), Kristian Dowling, 25 (bottom), Noam Galai, 21, Pascal Le Segretain, 12 (right), Scott Gries, 3 (top), 7, Steven Ferdman, 5: Aimee Todd, 3 (middle), 23, UPI/Phil McCarten, 8; Pixabay: 27707, background, GDJ, 12 (background)

ISBN: 978-1-62920-847-3 (library binding)
ISBN: 978-1-62920-859-6 (ePub)

Contents

	INTRODUCTION	4
Chapter 1	MEET THE JONASES	6
Chapter 2	JONAS BROTHERS HISTORY	10
Chapter 3	GOING SEPARATE WAYS	14
Chapter 4	JONAS FAMILY VALUES	18
Chapter 5	A LOOK AHEAD	22
	TIMELINE	26
	QUIZ	28
	ACTIVITY	29
	GLOSSARY	30
	READ MORE	31
	INTERNET SITES	31
	INDEX	32

Introduction

The Jonas Brothers are back! For six years, they did not perform. Kevin, Joe, and Nick worked on their own projects. But now the band is back together and hotter than ever.

On August 7, 2019, Kevin, Joe, and Nick Jonas took the stage at AmericanAirlines Arena. They were met with thunderous applause. It was the kickoff to their reunion tour.

The energetic welcome by the sold-out crowd proved that the pop rock band of brothers is back where it belongs. The family is together. They are creating crowd-pleasing songs. The band dropped its fifth studio album *Happiness Begins* on June 7, prior to the start of the reunion tour. Although the three brothers have successful solo careers, they still enjoy working together. Nick announced in 2020 that they are already working on a sixth Jonas Brothers album.

The 2019–20 Happiness Begins Tour featured new songs, as well as previous hits such as "S.O.S." and "Mandy."

Chapter 1

MEET THE JONASES

The Jonas brothers come from a humble family. They also have musical roots. Their father is Paul Kevin Jonas Sr. He is known as "Papa Jonas." Paul is a **minister**. Early in his career, he wrote and performed religious music.

Denise Miller-Jonas's nickname is "Mama Jonas." She joined her husband in making music. Denise also knows American Sign Language. Together, Paul and Denise had a music group called Signs of Love. They sang and signed each song.

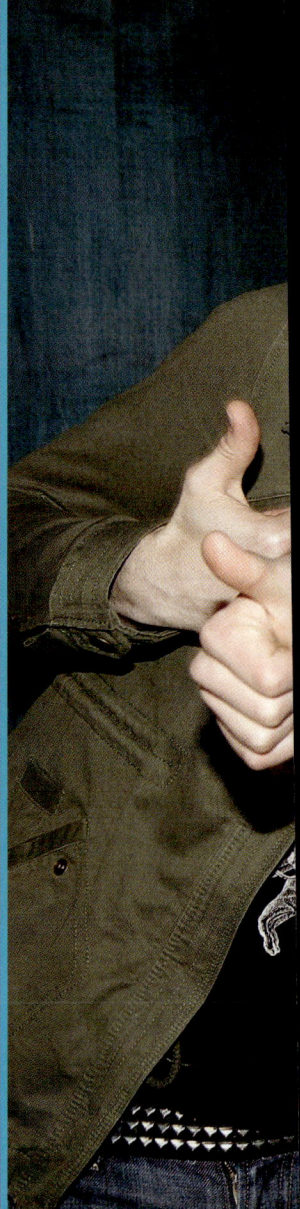

Famous Fact

Papa Jonas was accidentally hit with a guitar on set while his sons were filming the "Mandy" video. He needed three stitches to close the wound. "One for each of my boys," he said.

minister: a person who works as a leader at a church

Kevin, Nick, and Joe have always found time to goof around during their busy schedules.

For many years, Paul and Denise traveled for their work. Their sons were born in several different states. Kevin was born in 1987 in New Jersey. Joe was born two years later in Arizona. In 1992, Nick was born in Texas. The family finally settled down in the mid-1990s. They made their home in New Jersey. Before long, Paul and Denise had a fourth son, Frankie.

The Jonas family has always spent a lot of time together for work, school, and play.

Their new hometown was only about 20 minutes away from New York City. The family spent time visiting museums and other cultural attractions. Nick became interested in Broadway. He made it his goal to appear onstage. "From whenever I can remember, I've been telling my grandma I was going to be on Broadway," he once told a reporter.

Nick loved to sing all the time. Once, he was singing in a local barbershop while getting his hair cut. He was only six years old.

A person at the barbershop heard him. The person recommended a **talent agent** named Shirley Grant. Grant was impressed. She offered to represent the talented young boy. Thanks to his new agent, Nick was soon on stage and in TV commercials.

Kevin and Joseph also signed with Nick's agent. Soon they appeared in commercials too. They were for Burger King, Legos, and Chuck E. Cheese. Joe was also in an opera. He was 12 years old.

During this time, Denise started to **homeschool** the boys. She encouraged them to pursue their individual interests. It also gave them the freedom and flexibility to grow their musical careers.

talent agent: a person who helps find jobs for actors and other professionals in the entertainment industry

homeschool: a style of education where parents teach their children at home

FRANKIE JONAS

Kevin, Joe, and Nick's younger brother Frankie, who is not a member of the band, was in the 2009–10 show *Jonas*. Frankie even won a Teen Choice Award in 2009 for TV Breakout Male. All four brothers also appeared in the reality television show *Jonas Brothers: Living the Dream*. The show documented the band's life on the road.

Chapter 2

JONAS BROTHERS HISTORY

In 2003, Broadway performers were recording Christmas music. It was to raise money for AIDS research. AIDS is a sometimes-deadly disease that affects the blood. Nick was 12 years old. He decided to participate in the special project.

Instead of recording an existing song, Nick and his father Paul wrote a new one. They named it "Joy to the World (A Christmas Prayer)." The song lyrics are a call for "peace for every boy and girl, hope when life is hard, light when everything seems dark." Paul sent a **demo** of Nick's recording to a **record label**. The label **produced** Christian music. The song made its way to Christian radio stations. Then **executives** at Columbia Records heard Nick's song. They decided to sign him.

Famous Fact

The band name was supposed to be J3. The boys preferred the Jonas Brothers. Nick announced the name at their first concert, and the name stuck.

- - -

demo: a recording that a musician makes in order to show what their music is like

record label: a company that helps musical artists produce, promote, and sell their music

produce: to be in charge of creating and financing a creative project, such as a movie or music album

executive: a person who manages other people in a company

10 FAMILIES of Fame & Fortune

But Columbia Records didn't want Nick to sing Christian music. They had pop rock in mind for the young musician. They asked if Nick's brothers would join him. They could make up a new band. Kevin and Joseph jumped at the chance.

The Jonas Brothers won their first Nickelodeon Kids' Choice Awards for Favorite Music Group in 2008. They were nominated again in 2020.

Kevin, Joe, and Nick Jonas exploded onto the music scene in 2005. They released their first **single**, "Mandy." Their popularity got a huge boost in 2006. That was when the music video aired on MTV.

Jonas Family Tree

Paul Jonas
February 13, 1965
producer, songwriter, former minister

Denise Miller-Jonas
July 12, 1966
teacher

Paul Kevin Jonas Jr.
November 5, 1987
actor and musician

Danielle (Deleasa) Jonas
September 18, 1986
entrepreneur

Joseph Adam Jonas
August 15, 1989
actor and musician

Sophie Turner
February 21, 1996
actress

Willa Jonas
July 22, 2020

Alena Jonas
February 2, 2014

Valentina Jonas
October 27, 2016

Though their fame seemed to arrive suddenly, their path to success was rocky. They had their fair share of disappointments. Their fans adored them. But their record label wasn't convinced they had what it took to become very popular. Columbia Records dropped the band. The Jonas Brothers were left without a label.

They didn't give up. In 2007, Disney's record label, Hollywood, signed the band. The boys released their second album, *Jonas Brothers*.

This record brought them international fame. The band teamed up with the Disney Channel. They starred in their own television series in 2008. The show made "Jonas" a household name.

Nicholas Jerry Jonas
September 16, 1992
actor and musician

Priyanka Chopra
July 18, 1982
actress and singer

Franklin Nathaniel Jonas
September 28, 2000
actor and sound engineer

single: one song either released by itself, or as part of a larger musical album

entrepreneur: someone who starts a business and takes on large financial risk to do so

Chapter 3
GOING SEPARATE WAYS

The band enjoyed many years of fame and fortune. But in 2011, their careers began to change. Shows were not selling well. The brothers were making music they were not proud of. In 2013, they announced the band's breakup. Fans around the world were shocked.

Nick admits that he was behind the band's split. He said that he didn't feel that he and his brothers communicated well with each other. He wanted to explore solo projects.

At first, Kevin and Joe took the news hard. "I checked out in my mind—that was it. There's going to be no more brothers ever," Joe said in 2019. Nick added, "And I feared that, you know, they would never speak to me again."

Despite the difficult breakup, the boys used the time apart well. They pursued individual career goals and began families of their own.

Famous Fact

The band has released 5 full-length albums and sold more than 17 million copies worldwide as of 2020.

In the fall of 2013, the Jonas Brothers performed their final concert before breaking up.

Kevin and Danielle work on many charitable causes. In 2018, they promoted pet adoption during National Pet Month in May.

Kevin launched a real estate company. He also created a restaurant **app** called Yood. Kevin had married Danielle Deleasa in 2009. Danielle became a reality TV star. In her show, called *Married to Jonas*, she gave the world an inside look at being a part of the famous family. Danielle went on to lead many business **ventures**, including a jewelry company called Moments. Kevin concentrated on raising their two daughters.

Joe formed a pop rock group called DNCE. The band's hit single is "Cake by the Ocean." In 2016, Joe began dating Sophie Turner. Sophie became a star at a young age too. She was 14 when she started work on the TV show *Game of Thrones*.

app: a small computer program, usually downloaded to a mobile device
venture: a new project, business, or activity that usually involves risk

During the band's break, Nick performed with Nick Jonas and the Administration. He also met his future wife, Priyanka Chopra.

Priyanka is more famous in her home country of India than Nick is in the United States. Priyanka is multi-talented. She sings, acts, produces films, and is a model—all with great success.

Priyanka and Nick went on a date to the Golden Globe Awards in Beverly Hills, California, in 2020.

TAUGHT HIMSELF GUITAR

When he was young, Kevin stayed home sick from school for three days. He was only sick on the first day. Then he pretended to be ill. He spent the extra time teaching himself to play his father's guitar. In the band, Kevin plays lead guitar, rhythm guitar, and bass guitar. He also plays the mandolin, a kind of lute.

THE JONAS BROTHERS

Chapter 4

JONAS FAMILY VALUES

A health crisis helped bring the brothers back together. Papa Jonas was diagnosed with cancer in 2017. He fought the disease with his wife and their sons by his side. He is now in **remission**. In the end, the brothers decided family was the most important thing. They worked together to rebuild trust.

After six years apart, the brothers decided to come together again. At first, the plan was to make a **documentary**. It was going to be about their experiences as musicians and performers when they were teens. The plan started to grow. Then the brothers decided they wanted to do more than revisit the magic of their years in the band. They wanted to feel that magic again.

Famous Fact

In 2021, Nick was the host and musical guest on an episode of *Saturday Night Live*. He performed two new songs.

remission: a period of time during an illness when a person's health improves

documentary: a movie that presents real-life events and facts

Nick, Kevin, and Joe helped raise money for the Women's Cancer Research Fund at the Unforgettable Evening event in 2020.

For years, fans had been hoping for more music from the band of brothers. They finally got their wish. Ten years after their fourth album, they finally launched their fifth. *Happiness Begins* dropped in June 2019. Fans were thrilled to see 14 tracks with songs about love, life, and of course, happiness.

The Jonas Brothers have made a successful comeback. Their songs are at the top of the charts. Their music videos have millions of views. The brothers are hard at work to create and perform their new music.

While the brothers are used to fame, it is different this time. Joe, Nick, and Kevin are now learning to balance their jobs and their growing families. Joe and Nick now have support from their wives too.

Kevin and Danielle Jonas attended the Billboard Music Awards in 2019 together. The Jonas Brothers performed their hit "Sucker."

BEYOND TYPE 1

Nick Jonas suffers from type 1 diabetes. He was diagnosed with the disease in 2007, when he was 13. The condition made Nick lose weight and feel tired. This is because his blood sugar level was too high. Nick said he controls the disease by "working out and eating healthy and keeping my blood sugar in check." He founded a **nonprofit** organization. Beyond Type 1 supports people with the disease and funds research for a cure.

"Sucker" won an award for Best Pop Video at the 2019 MTV Video Music Awards. Sophie was there to share the event with Joe.

The trio of wives has been nicknamed the J Sisters. The J Sisters have joined their husbands in music videos. They first starred in "Sucker." In the video, the Jonas Brothers perform for their wives, who are dressed in **lavish** costumes. The video won an award for Best Pop Video. It was at the 2019 MTV Music Video Awards.

In early 2020, the partners released a video for "What a Man Gotta Do." For the video, the couples did different dance styles. Nick said, "It just felt right to have them involved. And they were kind enough to grace us with their presence. They're all very busy, so the fact that they were able to come do the video meant a lot to us."

nonprofit: a group or business that works toward a goal or purpose but does not make money doing so

lavish: fancy and seemingly expensive

Chapter 5
A LOOK AHEAD

As TV host Carson Daly said in 2020, the brothers have "the **Midas touch**" right now. Everything they work on turns to gold. Now that the band has reunited, fans can expect to see more creative **collaborations** between Kevin, Joe, and Nick. More music videos featuring the J Sisters might also be in store. They will pursue solo projects as well. In 2020, Nick started appearing as a judge on *The Voice*.

Frankie Jonas was too young to perform in the band when it first started. But fans will likely see more of him now. He has been pursuing a career of his own. He has worked as a **voice actor** since 2009. In 2019, he began writing and producing music. Frankie became popular on TikTok in 2020. He has almost 2 million followers on the app.

Midas touch: the ability to make every project successful

collaboration: working with another person or group in order to achieve a goal

voice actor: an actor who uses their voice and not their face for a production, such as animated films and TV shows

The final leg of the Happiness Begins Tour was in Europe, with stops in the United Kingdom, Germany, Spain, and France.

— *Famous Fact* —

Nick Jonas released his fourth solo album, *Spaceman*, on March 12, 2021. The album features a song called "Selfish," which is a collaboration with Kevin and Joe.

The brothers are growing their families as well as their careers. In 2019, Joe and Sophie shocked their fans with a surprise wedding. The couple welcomed their first baby in 2020. Sophie is hard at work on her acting career. This includes a new thriller TV show called *Survive*. Sophie plays a plane crash survivor. Joe has a part in a movie about the Korean War called *Devotion*.

In 2017 and 2019, Nick returned to the silver screen. He was in the first two films of the *Jumanji* **reboot**. He had roles in a science fiction movie and a TV show in 2021. Nick also released a new song called "Superman" in 2021. Priyanka is breaking into American **media** as well. "I realized that South Asian actors get put into a box . . . So I thought, the way to make a dent would be to not play Indian characters at all," she said. She starred in a superhero movie in 2020. It was called *We Can Be Heroes*.

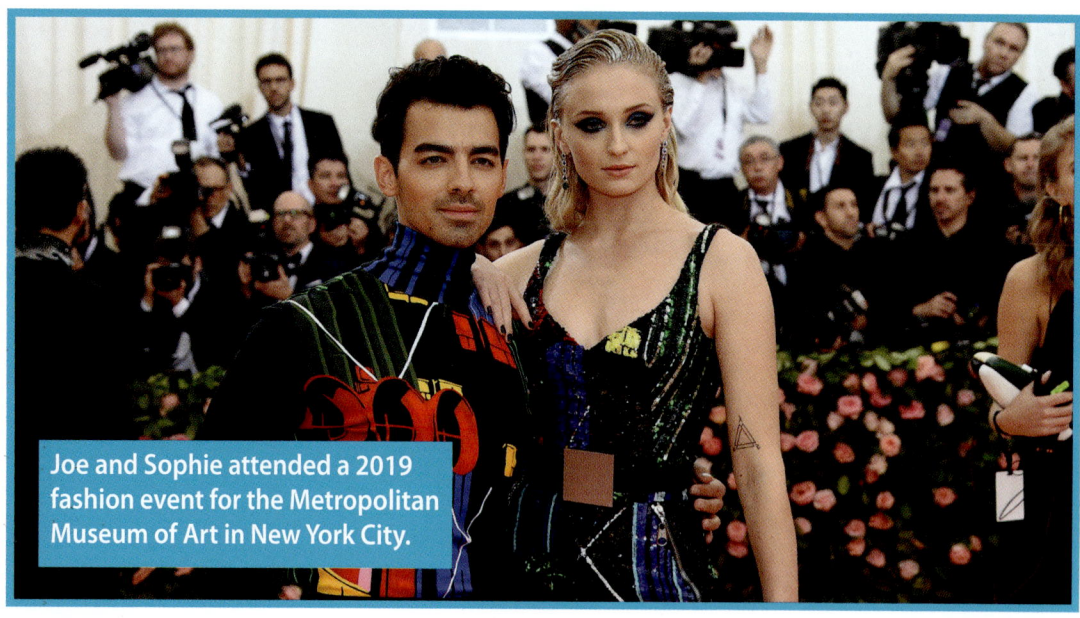

Joe and Sophie attended a 2019 fashion event for the Metropolitan Museum of Art in New York City.

reboot: a remake or revival of an old series

media: the ways people receive information and see creative works, including radio stations, TV stations, and newspapers

Danielle continues to work on her jewelry business. She and Kevin recently celebrated their 11th wedding anniversary. The entire family has been traveling with Kevin during the Happiness Begins tour.

Life as rock stars has not always been easy. But these brothers have learned the importance of working on their own individual goals and following their own passions. Fans can look forward to the best of both solo and group projects from this talented family.

Kevin and Danielle, as well as the other Jo Bros and J Sisters, attended the 2020 Grammy Awards in Los Angeles, California.

FOLLOW THE JONASES

Fans love following the Jonases on social media. The brothers have millions of followers on Instagram and Twitter. They share posts about performing and about their families. Kevin's pictures of his two young daughters earn hundreds of thousands of likes. Even mom Denise Miller-Jonas has gotten into the social media act. She has more than 300,000 followers on Instagram as of May 2021.

THE JONAS BROTHERS   25

Timeline

2005

Kevin, Joe, and Nick Jonas form a band. They name it the Jonas Brothers.

2007

Danielle meets Kevin during a family vacation in the Bahamas. She hadn't heard of the Jonas Brothers.

2008

The brothers appear on the Disney Channel in *Camp Rock*. Two years later, *Camp Rock 2: The Final Jam* is released.

2016
Sophie Turner wins her first major solo awards, a Glamour Award and an EWwy Award, for her work on *Game of Thrones*.

2021
The Jonas Brothers record "Selfish" on Nick's fourth solo album *Spaceman*, released in March 2021.

2017
Forbes lists Priyanka as one of the World's 100 Most Powerful Women. She makes the list a second time in 2018.

2012
The band begins working together on a new album and a possible tour. The next year, the band decides to break up.

Quiz

1. Where was Nick when a talent agent heard him sing?

2. What was the band supposed to be called?

3. In what year did they announce the band's breakup?

4. What kind of work does Priyanka do?

5. On what app did Frankie have almost 2 million followers in 2021?

6. When did Sophie win her first major solo awards?

1. A barbershop
2. J13
3. 2013
4. She sings, acts, produces films, and is a model.
5. TikTok
6. 2016

Activity

The Jonas Brothers were raised in a musical and creative family. You don't have to live in a musical family to learn about musical instruments. There are many ways to explore music and learn to be creative.

MATERIALS

- pen and pencil
- local newspaper
- internet access
- helpful adult

STEPS

1. Make a list of your favorite songs. Create a playlist and listen.
2. Pay attention to the parts of the songs you like best. Did you enjoy the drum solo? The bass guitar section? The soaring lead singer or the back-up vocals?
3. Use your experiences with your favorite music to decide which aspect of music you would like to explore.
4. With the help of a trusted adult, visit a local music store. Ask the store owner questions about the instruments. Which instrument would the store owner recommend for a beginner? Do they lend instruments to new students? Is the instrument expensive? Is it difficult to keep the instrument in good repair?
5. Check online for information about local music teachers. Email or call to ask questions about lessons and fees.
6. With a parent's permission, take a class. Decide if you want to pursue learning your instrument. Share your music with your family and friends!

Glossary

app: a small computer program, usually downloaded to a mobile device

collaboration: working with another person or group in order to achieve a goal

demo: a recording that a musician makes in order to show what their music is like

documentary: a movie that presents real-life events and facts

entrepreneur: someone who starts a business and takes on large financial risk to do so

executive: a person who manages other people in a company

homeschool: a style of education where parents teach their children at home

lavish: fancy and seemingly expensive

media: the ways people receive information and see creative works, including radio stations, TV stations, and newspapers

Midas touch: the ability to make every project successful

minister: a person who works as a leader at a church

nonprofit: a group or business that works toward a goal or purpose, but does not make money doing so

produce: to be in charge of creating and financing a creative project, such as a movie or music album

reboot: a remake or revival of an old series

record label: a company that helps musical artists produce, promote, and sell their music

remission: a period of time during an illness when a person's health improves

single: one song either released by itself, or as part of a larger musical album

talent agent: a person who helps find jobs for actors and other professionals in the entertainment industry

venture: a new project, business, or activity that usually involves risk

voice actor: an actor who uses their voice and not their face for a production, such as animated films and TV shows

Read More

Careers: The Graphic Guide to Planning Your Future. New York: DK Children, 2015.

Krull, Kathleen. *Frenemies in the Family: Famous Brothers and Sisters Who Butted Heads and Had Each Other's Backs.* New York: Crown, 2018.

Mackenzie, Malcolm. *Idols of Pop: The Jonas Brothers.* New York: HarperCollins, 2020.

Toren, Adam. *Starting Your Own Business: Become an Entrepreneur!* Hoboken, NJ: John Wiley & Sons Inc., 2017.

Walker, Carolina. *You Can Work in Music.* You Can Work in the Arts. North Mankato, MN.: Capstone Press, 2018.

Internet Sites

Camp Rock
Learn more about the Jonas Brothers' first Disney movie.
https://wiki.kidzsearch.com/wiki/Camp_Rock

Jonas Brothers Biography
Read biographical information about the brothers and their band.
https://www.ducksters.com/biography/jonas_brothers.php

Joy Tunes Blog
Explore different instruments and decide which you would like to play.
http://www.joytunes.com/blog/learn-to-play/instrument-learn-play

Index

agents 8, 9
awards 9, 11, 17, 20, 21, 25, 27

Beyond Type 1 20
Broadway 8, 10

Chopra, Priyanka 13, 17, 24, 27
Columbia Records 10, 11, 13

Disney 13, 26
DNCE 16
documentaries 18

Happiness Begins 4, 19
Happiness Begins Tour 5, 23, 25

Jonas, Danielle (Deleasa) 12, 16, 20, 25, 26
Jonas, Frankie (Franklin) 7, 9, 13, 22
Jonas, Joe (Joseph) 4, 7, 9, 11, 12, 14, 16, 19, 20, 21, 22, 24, 26
Jonas, Kevin 4, 7, 9, 11, 12, 14, 16, 17, 19, 20, 22, 25, 26
Jonas, Nick 4, 7, 8, 9, 10, 11, 12, 13, 14, 17, 19, 20, 21, 22, 24, 26
Jonas Sr., Paul Kevin "Papa Jonas" 6, 7, 10, 12, 18
J Sisters 21, 22, 25

Miller-Jonas, Denise "Mama Jonas" 6, 7, 9, 12, 25

singles 12, 16
social media 25

Turner, Sophie 12, 16, 21, 24, 27

The Voice 22